LUCIE *the* HIPPO

TERELL *the* TURTLE

CLEO *the* SOW

GOLDIE *the* GOOSE

HAROLD *the* HORSE

OSWALD *the* OWL

MISS FISHER *the* FLAMINGO

CHESTER *the* BASSETT HOUND

PRINCIPAL CECIL *the* GOAT

LUCIE *the* HIPPO

GOLDIE *the* GOOSE

STEWART *the* GIRAFFE

BELVA *the* HEIFER

BELVA *the* HEIFER

MRS. HIPPO

WINSTON *the* RABBIT

CHESTER *the* BASSETT HOUND

PRINCIPAL CECIL *the* GOAT

CLEO *the* SOW

HAROLD *the* HORSE

TERELL *the* TURTLE

LUCIE *the* HIPPO

TO MY FAMILY

Who helped me see how to
"make all my mountains into a road."

~ Isaiah 49:11

Scripture quotation has been taken from the Holman Christian Standard Bible®, Copyright© 1999, 2000, 2002, 2003 by Holman Bible Publishers. Used by permission. Holman Christian Standard Bible®, Holman CSB®, and HCSB® are federally registered trademarks of Holman Bible Publishers.

look at me; i am just like you

Published by:
Pecan Row Press
www.pecanrowpress.com
Email: info@pecanrowpress.com

Printed in China

Library of Congress Cataloging – in – Publication Data

Hardin, Abigail Cole
    Look At Me; I Am Just Like You / by Abigail Cole Hardin

ISBN – 13: 978-0-9795187-1-3

ISBN – 10: 0-9795187-1-7

Illustrator: Stacie Schneeflock
Graphic Designer: Stacie Schneeflock

look at me; i am just like you

abigail cole hardin

illustrated by stacie schneeflock

Pecan Row Press
JACKSON, MISSISSIPPI 39216
www.pecanrowpress.com

It was Lucie the Hippo's first day at Barnaby Elementary School. She was so excited finally to know what her new school was like. She couldn't wait to meet her new classmates. However, Lucie did not know how hard it would be for her to adjust. She was soon to find out that school was not what she hoped it would be.

Lucie did not realize how different she looked from most hippopotamuses. She was born with a purple smudge on her cheek that resembled the shape of a pineapple. It was her birthmark, and because it had always been there, she never thought much about it— until she arrived at school.

The bell rang, and class began. Lucie's attention was caught by an older pink flamingo lady with big round spectacles who stood at the front of the classroom. With a booming voice, the flamingo said, "Good morning, class. I am your teacher, Miss Fisher. I am so excited to announce that we have a new student with us today. Will Lucie the Hippo please come up front with me?"

Lucie quickly got up from her desk and walked toward Miss Fisher, but before she could say anything, the flamingo's eyes became as big as donuts!

*M*iss Fisher gasped and said, "Oh my goodness! Are you alright?" Lucie was confused by her teacher's reaction because she felt fine.

Miss Fisher continued, "Sweetie, did you get hit in the face? That looks like it hurts!"

Before Lucie could explain that it was her birthmark, the whole class roared with laughter and gave her questioning looks. Lucie's whole face turned red, as she saw all of her classmates staring and pointing at her. **She felt like she didn't belong because of her birthmark. Everyone looked at her like she was different.** Miss Fisher tried to get the class to settle down, but the laughter continued.

A goose named Goldie shouted out to Lucie, "What kind of hippopotamuses have big ink blots on their faces?"

Then a big sow named Cleo chimed in, "So what did you do, fall on your face?" The goose and the sow cackled and snorted until Miss Fisher silenced the class.

Tears streamed down Lucie's face. Miss Fisher looked at Lucie and said, "Oh, Lucie, I am so sorry that I upset you! I was concerned. Can you tell me and the class what happened?"

Lucie blurted out, "It's just a birthmark! I'm fine!"

Suddenly, the whole class started whispering. They continued to stare at her. Lucie felt ashamed of the way she looked. She began to wish she had never gone to school.

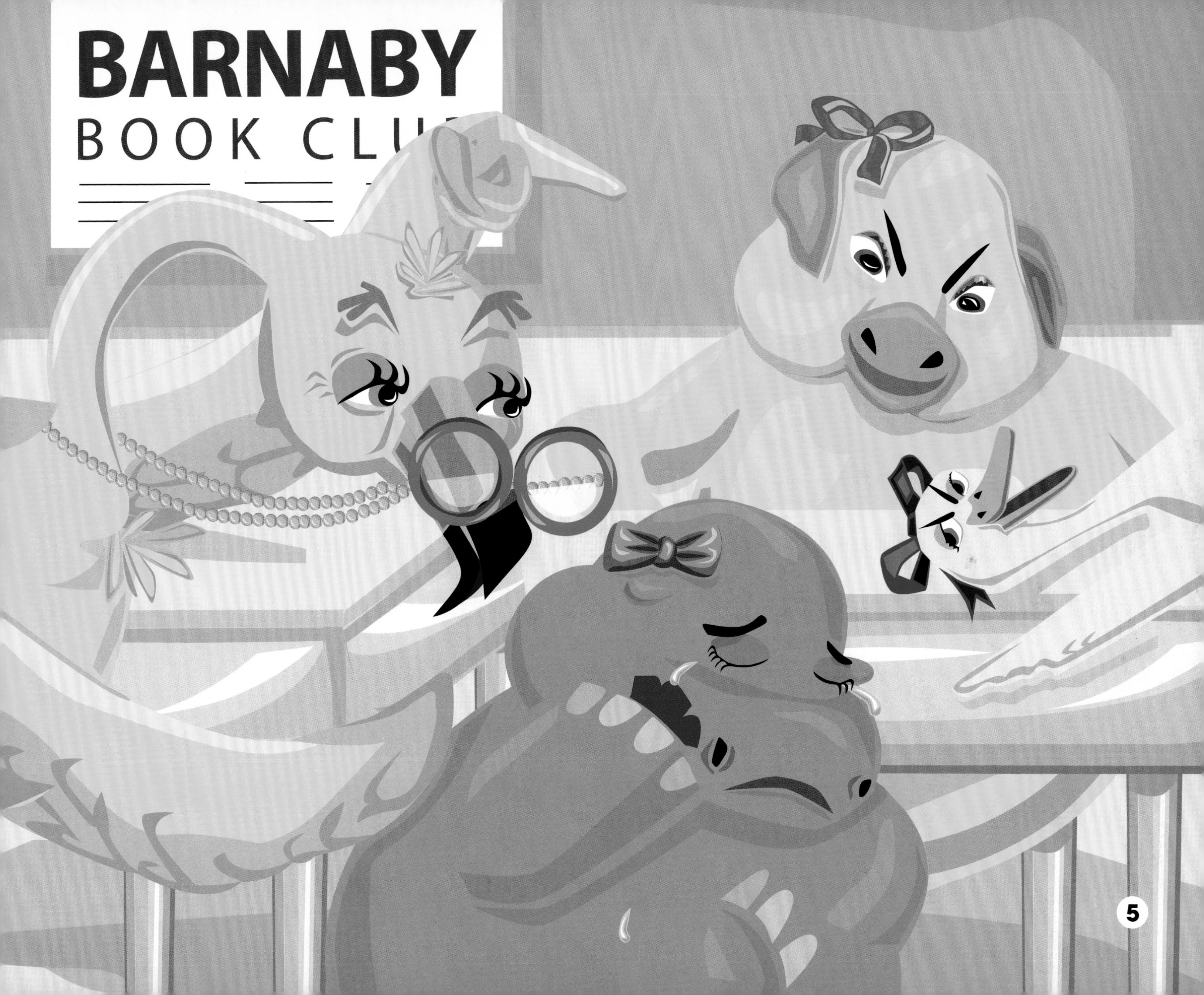
BARNABY
BOOK CLU

After a long day at school, Lucie the Hippo, with the pineapple birthmark, arrived back at her house and went inside. Her mother, Mrs. Hippo, greeted her with a huge smile and asked, "So how was your first day at school, Lucie?"

Lucie snapped back, "I never want to go back to school again!"

Her mom was shocked and asked, "Why, Lucie? What happened?"

Lucie continued, "No one likes me because of my birthmark. They all thought I got hit in the face—even my teacher! I don't belong there. I look too different. I just wish I was invisible, so no one would stare at me."

Mrs. Hippo looked comfortingly at her daughter and said, "Lucie, I know you may feel that way, but you don't need to hide. Your birthmark is what makes you special, not different. Your teacher and classmates probably don't understand what it's like to have a birthmark, so it does not mean that they don't like you. I think you should give them another chance. Show them what a great friend you can be. Just be yourself, and remember— no one is the same. **We all have something that makes us different from the other. Having differences is actually one of the important ways we are all alike.** So tell them, *"Look at me; I am just like you."*

The next day, Lucie the Hippo, with the pineapple birthmark, got up enough courage to go back to Barnaby Elementary School. She made sure she sat in the back of the classroom, so no one would notice her. Lucie observed her classmates. A very smart owl named Oswald was answering all the questions. However, a giraffe, whom Lucie had not noticed until now, timidly raised his hand.

Goldie the Goose shouted out, "Stewart, put your hand down. You take too long to answer because you st-st-stttutter."

The whole class, except Stewart and Lucie, started laughing at Goldie's comment. They began imitating Stewart by talking more slowly than usual. Lucie was upset the class was making fun of him because she knew he couldn't help his stuttering, just as she couldn't help having a birthmark. She saw that Stewart was about to cry.

Lucie really wanted to go up to Stewart and say, "*Look at me; I am just like you.* It's okay to be different." **But she didn't because she was still too afraid about being different herself and too worried what the class might think about her.**

After the lesson had ended, Miss Fisher turned to the class and said, "Students, I have an announcement to make. The annual Barnaby Elementary School spelling bee competition is this week. Our class will compete against students within the same grade. It is the biggest event of the school year because the winning class from each grade wins an ice cream party and a field trip to the Wet 'N' Wild Water Park!"

The whole class cheered. Goldie the Goose shouted out, "We're going to win! We have Oswald the Owl on our team!"

Miss Fisher chuckled, and sternly said, "The number one rule for the spelling bee competition is that everyone must participate. The hardest words will be towards the end of the competition, so carefully plan the order in which your classmates compete. Whichever class spells the most words correctly wins the ice cream party and the field trip. Therefore, the best way to win is by working together as a team and encouraging your classmates."

Suddenly, the bell rang for recess, and Miss Fisher dismissed the class.

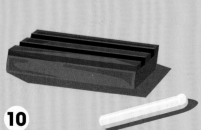

When Lucie reached the playground, she saw her classmates huddled up around Goldie the Goose, who was thinking of a team plan to win the spelling bee competition. "Oswald is the best speller in our class," Goldie explained, "so he should be the last one to spell because he will compete against Winston the Rabbit, who is the best in the other class."

The crowd agreed. Goldie continued, "We need the best spellers towards the end, so, Cleo the Sow, you'll be before Oswald. Then Chester the Basset Hound, you're before Cleo. Then me, then Belva the Heifer, and then you, ole 'Turtle head,' and then let me see. *Hmmm...*"

Goldie instructed the crowd in the order she thought was best. Lucie the Hippo was second in the order, which made her feel like she wasn't smart enough to spell the harder words towards the end. **Even though Lucie could spell very well, no one knew because she never spoke up.**

"Okay, I think that's it," said Goldie.

"W-w-wait! W-what about mm-m-me?"

The crowd started laughing. Cleo the Sow replied, "Stewart, you can't even speak, so what makes you think you can spell? You're going to make us lose if you're in the competition."

Stewart put his head down. He wished he was invisible.

13

"**N**o, he *has* to be in it!" Lucie protested. "Remember what Miss Fisher said? Everyone has to be in it."

Goldie answered, "Oh, great. Stewart, you'd better not come to school the day of the spelling bee. I don't want to lose the competition because of you."

The crowd agreed with Goldie, and Stewart felt sad that no one wanted him. **Again, Lucie wanted to take up for him, but she was still too afraid.**

It was the day of the annual Barnaby Elementary School spelling bee competition. Lucie the Hippo was about to walk into the building when she saw Stewart the Giraffe being bullied by her classmates. They were angry he had come to school because they believed they would not win the spelling bee if he competed. Lucie the Hippo did not know what to do. She was too afraid to help Stewart.

All of a sudden, Stewart the Giraffe ran away from his classmates and headed toward the bushes behind the school building. School was about to start, and Lucie knew she needed to go to class.

15

When Lucie reached the classroom, Miss Fisher the Flamingo was taking roll.

"Goldie the Goose?"

"Here," said Goldie.

"Stewart the Giraffe?" The class was silent. Miss Fisher continued, "Stewart?" There was still no answer. "Where's Stewart today?"

The class began looking at each other. Everyone was afraid to tell where he was. It was up to Lucie to tell the truth, but would she find the courage to stand up for Stewart? Would she overcome her fear of what her classmates might think of her? **Would she accept being different?**

Stewart
Lucie
Goldie
Cleo
Oswald
Chester

All of a sudden, Lucie the Hippo raised her hand and said, "I think I know why Stewart isn't here." The whole class glared at her, but she continued, "Miss Fisher, Stewart ran away."

"Why?" exclaimed the flamingo.

Lucie struggled to tell her. She thought she couldn't go on. Then, for the first time, she stopped being afraid. "I think Stewart's feelings were hurt. He was told not to come to school today because his stuttering would make our class lose the spelling bee."

Goldie the Goose looked at Lucie angrily, but Lucie kept talking.

"You see, Miss Fisher, I know how Stewart feels. I know that I am different because of my birthmark, and like Stewart, it is hard for me to feel like I belong,...and Miss Fisher...I don't think we will win the spelling bee unless we work together as a team and include Stewart. We all have something that makes us different from one another, but that is not bad. It is bad when we are mean to those who are different. If we can learn to see how we are alike, then we won't leave anyone out. **So even though I look different on the outside, I'm just the same because I want to be liked and included like you do.** *Look at me; I am just like you."*

Goldie the Goose wanted to argue with Lucie, but she saw the others were listening to the hippo. Goldie looked down, ashamed, then stood up and said softly, "You're right, Lucie. I left you and Stewart out. I'm sorry for being mean and hurting your feelings. I want to find Stewart. It's my fault he ran away."

Lucie replied, "No, Goldie, it's not just your fault. We all saw Stewart as different, and none of us took up for him. We all need to apologize."

Miss Fisher broke in, "Well let's go find Stewart before it's too late!"

There wasn't much time before the spelling bee competition would begin, but Miss Fisher's class was determined to find Stewart. They searched the playground, but Stewart wasn't there. They searched the bushes, but Stewart wasn't there. They searched in the garbage cans, but Stewart wasn't there either.

The class started losing hope until, suddenly, they heard someone crying behind the building. The class rushed over to Stewart the Giraffe who was hiding in a pile of tires with tears streaming down his face.

ucie the Hippo ran to him and said, "Thank goodness we found you! We were all so worried. We want to apologize to you, Stewart. We realized we left you out because you stutter, but stuttering is nothing to be sad about. **We all have something that makes us different, but we all have feelings that make us the same.**"

Stewart looked down sadly. He didn't want to talk because he was still ashamed of his stuttering. Then, Lucie spoke up and said what she had wanted to say to him from the first time she saw his feelings get hurt. *"Look at me, Stewart; I am just like you."*

The class cheered and apologized to Stewart. Goldie the Goose gave Stewart a huge hug. She promised never to make fun of him again. Stewart the Giraffe smiled and felt better than ever.

Then Miss Fisher announced, "We've got to hurry or we won't make it in time for the competition. Since Stewart didn't have a place in the order of competition, he'll have to go last."

"Oh n-no!" exclaimed Stewart.

Then Lucie looked at him and said, "Stewart, we don't care if you misspell or stutter. As long as you're a part of our team and do your best, we know we have already won."

The whole class agreed and promised to cheer him on. Miss Fisher's class was now ready for the spelling bee competition.

The spelling bee was down to its last contestants, Winston the Rabbit, who was the best speller in the other class, and Stewart the Giraffe.

Principal Cecil the Goat, with a long gray beard, faced the audience and announced that whoever spelled the last word correctly would win the competition.

Stewart was very nervous until he heard his class cheering for him and encouraging him to do his best. The last word to spell was "pageant." Stewart the Giraffe couldn't even say the first letter before Winston the Rabbit blurted out the letters, "P-A-J-E— *wait! I mean G!*" But it was too late.

It was Stewart's turn. "p-P. A. jj-G. E. A. nn-N. t-t-T?"

The principal looked at Stewart and said, "That is correct. You just won the spelling bee!"

The crowd went wild. Miss Fisher's class ran on stage and gathered around Stewart. They were all so excited about winning. **They realized Stewart's slower way of talking made him take his time and spell the word correctly.** Principal Cecil brought out the big trophy and congratulated Stewart.

The next day, Principal Cecil visited Miss Fisher's classroom. "I have a special award for this class. In all these years at Barnaby Elementary School, I have never seen a class show as much teamwork as all of you did. Therefore, I want to present to you the 'Best Teamwork Award'." The class cheered! The principal smiled and asked, "I just want to know how you worked together so well?"

The class shouted, "It was Lucie! Lucie the Hippo showed us!"

Principal Cecil looked at Lucie, who explained, **"We worked together so well because we learned to look past the differences we all have and accept each other for who we are.** That's how we stopped leaving each other out and started working together as a team. We all want to be liked and included, so we made sure everyone felt accepted."

Stewart shouted out, "And we w-wouldn't have won and worked as a t-team if it wasn't for Lucie! Hip-hip-hooray for the hippo!"

The class joined in. "Hip-hip-hooray for the hippo!" Lucie blushed, then smiled, because she finally overcame her fear about being different. As a result, she was able to help Stewart gain confidence in himself and win the spelling bee. She also helped her class learn how to be sensitive to those who are different, which helped them receive the "Best Teamwork Award".

ucie also wants to encourage you that whenever you feel different from others, **look at her; she is just like you!**